Sedley

Sedley poems

Chelsea Coupal

COTEAU BOOKS

Edited by Bruce Rice
Designed by Tania Craan
Cover art by Jeff Nye, "The Pink House", oil on canvas, 2012
Printed and bound in Canada

Library and Archives Canada Cataloguing in Publication

Coupal, Chelsea, author
Sedley : poems / Chelsea Coupal.

Issued in print and electronic formats.
ISBN 978-1-55050-941-0 (softcover).--ISBN 978-1-55050-942-7 (PDF)

COTEAU BOOKS

2517 Victoria Avenue
Regina, Saskatchewan
Canada S4P 0T2
www.coteaubooks.com

Available in Canada from:
Publishers Group Canada
2440 Viking Way
Richmond, British Columbia
Canada V6V 1N2

10 9 8 7 6 5 4 3 2 1

Coteau Books gratefully acknowledges the financial support of its publishing program by: the Saskatchewan Arts Board, The Canada Council for the Arts, the Government of Saskatchewan through Creative Saskatchewan, the City of Regina. We further acknowledge the [financial] support of the Government of Canada. Nous reconnaissons l'appui [financier] du gouvernement du Canada.

Saskatchewan Arts Board
Canada Council for the Arts / Conseil des Arts du Canada
Canada
Government of Saskatchewan

Table of Contents

Cinnamon, smoke and the sulphur spark

First Day

We smell Fall before we see it:
cinnamon, smoke, the sulphur spark
of a match. We already see

bonfires we will lean toward
with kids who live just down
the highway from us.

I believe this year I will learn the curve
of someone else's body, wrap it around
my own like a comma; will stamp some part

of myself onto someone else, permanent
as a cigarette burn – stubborn, round reminder.
But right now, we're friends

drinking in pin-sharp daylight, a bright sky
blank as our first-day
notebooks. Ashley sits beside me

in sunglasses, cigarette thin as herself
in one hand, beer in the other, dark hair
tumbling over her shoulders. She is the smartest

and the hardest partyer – we call her *Rebel-Nerd.*
I have known her since the day before kindergarten.
We zip through the Teddy Bear Hills,

where prairie arches its back. CDs, shiny as diamonds,
line the visors. Kristy plucks one, slips it in.
Sheryl Crow sings *Strong Enough*

so we turn it up and sing,
louder and louder, our voices lying
on top of each other. Embellished air:

dust flecks reflecting
like sequins. Home by supper,
the drive a secret I clutch

like a stolen peach, hold up to my face later
in private, run the fuzz of its skin
across my lips, then rip in.

A Plain Run

I run at dusk, over gravel and stones,
glance at red waves that rip through the sky.
Under my feet a crunch like bones.
Everywhere wind, a songbird, a sigh.

Glance at red waves that rip through the sky,
wash over flax fields, lavender sand.
Here is wind, a songbird, a sigh
as day's breath sips cold at my hand.

Red waves wash over flax fields, lavender sand.
A doe in the ditch stands bone-still and stares
as the day's breath sips cold at my hand
and the foals in the pasture nudge at the mares.

A doe in the ditch stands bone-still and stares.
My lungs, breathless shells, tap at my chest
while the foals in the pasture nudge at the mares.
They graze on the grass, feast without rest.

My lungs, breathless shells, tap at my chest.
Under my feet a crunch like bones.
The mares graze on grass, feast without rest.
I run at dusk, over gravel and stones.

The full moon, a yard light

over the house surrounded by long grass
and tall Caragana bushes. This house –
a corpse returning itself to soil

slowly. While we still can, we visit
again and again, think of our own
rotting bodies, what they might do if left empty.

Watch for nails, we say, as if we can see
beyond the dust floating slow
as ocean plankton in the paths

of our flashlights. First you think of falling
through the wooden floor, then of the family
who lived here: a mother washing clothes

and rocking babies, hoping for a better year,
praying. Now every surface is dirt-smothered
and covered in mouse shit, and despite the wind

sneaking in through glassless windows, there's a skunk smell.
And a bathtub in the middle of the kitchen. Shattered amber
glass from those who trespassed before us: last weekend

or last year, it's impossible to tell. A barn swallow's
abandoned nest, fallen feathers curled like petals
on the floor. Passing cigarettes and Pilsner,

we yip like puppies, frightened and excited. When we leave,
we bring our bottles with us, glance back at the place, shape
of a bison, outlined in moonlight against the horizon.

Ms. Douglas

Youngest teacher at Sedley High, plans
to commute from Regina, but the school board
says *no*. So she rents a sunburnt shack – paint hanging

off it – on the town's edge, a house that reminds her
of herself, tough and thin as a tumbleweed.
Everyone curious about this tall, 22-year-old nobody

has ever seen before, unmarried. It is 1980 and
school has just started. The boys can't stand her
telling them how to serve a volleyball.

They hide dead mice in her desk, string up
jackrabbits on her front porch. The bachelors
want to cut her grass, wash her car. Every time

she runs, two or three stop to offer a ride, surprised
to hear she wants the exercise. One man, drunk, knocks
on her door late Saturday night, asks if he can

come in to chat about school matters, since he sits
on the board. She lets him in, makes tea, then
sends him on his wobbly way. He sleeps in his car

and doesn't wake until next day, half the parish
dressed in lace and beige, breezing past his Cadillac,
the sun falling slow as honey through his windows.

Ms. Douglas meets her future husband, my father,
at the town's only tavern one afternoon after school.
(The whole place lives in mist, everything soaked

in booze and smoke and stale breath.) She asks Sandra:
Who's that? and nods toward a man black-haired
and tanned. *That's my brother*, she says, laughs.

Some girls think he's handsome,
but honestly, don't go out with him.
He's an asshole.

Suzy-Marie

Sometimes kids showed up in the yearbook once – then left, ghosts,
thin-wispy as smoke. They blew in like seeds caught in a cold breeze.

We attacked like coyotes. Suzy-Marie with a zee
and a hyphen was one drifter kid. Grade 4. Her ponytail a long,
  blond rope

she wrapped around her neck sometimes. And her clothes were off.
One afternoon, November, she wore a fuchsia jumpsuit under
  sweatpants –

just hot pink stretched over her chest, a slick second skin.
It's too cold out there today for swimsuits, our teacher said, his voice
  dirt-dry.

That year our school put on a Christmas toy bingo at the town hall.
Best prize was a real CD player with removable speakers. I sat with the
  same girls

I'd sat with since kindergarten – Kristy, Ashley and Jill. And guess who
  won the stereo?
We were all shocked, mouths dropped, murmuring to each other. After
  the holidays,

teachers asked us over and over what we got and every time she said:
the new Spice Girls CD. Every time, she said it. Behind cupped palms,
  we whispered:

Is that all she got? She didn't speak to anyone except our teacher
and my friends with older sisters accused her of flirting. We were nine

but knew these things, although we still wore hoodies with puppy dogs
on them, and shoes with Velcro, too. A year older than us, she wore a bra

that showed beneath her shirt sometimes, and we accused her
of stuffing it with tissue. I think she left that summer.

When she didn't come back, we didn't notice,
or just didn't say anything – all of us grateful. She was gone.

Week One

Grade 9, only three years,
eight months, twenty-
one days to go.
Wish to skim
off some part
of yourself, shed
your skin in one
smooth curve, thin
petal of flesh. Cuticles
picked into slim blood
lines, hard sharp scratch
at the back of your
throat, hope for the bell
to hit 3:30 soon, escape.

This wish hangs, tangled
as wet hair, ropy, slick
as a seal. It stings, too,
like a long breath-hold,
one length of the pool,
lonely trip in clear
chlorine.

                    Underneath, blue-
green glow and a drain passes,
a Band-aid, grate, another drain, dropped
ear plug, lost bobby pin. All
the way to the other side
until fingertips, white-wrinkled
as bedsheets, touch
concrete and you shatter

the surface, gasp, pant, chest
pressed tight against your
suit, brick-heavy and hard
as a stone fist.

And the mind
cradling you like a mother: *You're ok.*
You're ok. You're ok.

The Divide

(Living Room)
Fresh moms bounce plump
babies on young

laps. Someone's bride, still wedding-gown slim, passes
out a house plan, points

at the optional bathroom.
Someone asks about low
flow toilets.

Their fingers boast mini
diamonds that peek and shine

like fillings. I gulp down another whiskey
coke, glance at my wristwatch.

A boy locked on his mother's knee
coos, blows
spit bubbles my way.

Are you still in school
or working now? his mother asks.

(Kitchen)
The guys grab
Pilsners.

Talk about rain, the price of canola
senior hockey and tractors.

Their amber bottles and
double-negatives clink.

The wives trickle in at half
past twelve. The babies need their cribs.
So hurry.

A cake tucked under
too much frosting waits

to be sliced. I imagine resting
my face in the sugar
soaked topping.

(Bedroom)
I wanted to leave ages
ago, but I spread anyway

like a colt. He slides his hands down
my body and murmurs
You're so gorgeous.

Morning, I wake, alone.
Next moment he's bedside, holding

a baby plate, a bagel, cream
cheese and strawberries.

I thank him. He leaves me
in bed. He has to
spray his lentils.

Sestina For The Party

I glance at my shoes covered in dirt and dust
and drink warm beer from a plastic cup.
Someone pulls up a truck blaring music.
We don't know the guys from these towns,
where we're sure hicks and inbreds live.
(Turns out the towns are exactly the same.)

We all drive grid roads; we all dress the same.
Nervous, I make a dull rainbow in dust
with my shoe. Wonder if this is how all kids live,
then look at Jill as she looks in her cup.
We hardly know anyone from these next-door towns.
He stands near the truck, bobs his head. Music

plays. God-and-corn-and-good-woman music,
the kind most of us like. The same
stuff our parents liked, raised in towns
we cruise now, windows down, spitting dust
at anyone walking. He fills my cup,
smiles, then speaks: *You lush, you know how to live,*

don't you? I laugh and tell him that *I live*
the only way I know how. Music
plays. He takes my hand and throws his cup
on the ground. We dance the same
way. Shuffle, drag our feet through dust
and name our small towns.

French and Russian names, these towns.
Places our grandparents used to live,
before they gave birth in all of this dust.
He asks if I like the music.
I don't like country. It all sounds the same,
I say as I sip from my cup.

He turns to the keg on the truck, fills his cup,
looks for his friends from other towns.
I don't like Sedley girls. They all look the same.
He says he's kidding, says I should *live*
a little. I do dance to the music,
slide my feet on brown ground, plain dust.

I sip from my cup, share the dust
with kids from different towns. We sway to the music
the same sort of way, wondering how we should live.

The Near-Death Drive

The truck's lodged along the dugout's slope
at an unnerving angle, like a broken wrist.
We finally have a story to polish and hold
out to our friends, bright-ripe as an apple.
This will be a whole event. Someone
will have to save us. Someone will
have to tow out the truck. But our cells
don't have service, so we walk along
back roads, our mud-soaked shoes
heavy as hooves. The closest farmyard a pinprick
of white light. Pulses throbbing,
urging us forward: *Go on, go on, go on.*
Northern lights waver, a silent music
we can see. And once in a while
our own laughter bursts through
like roman candles, sharp and sparkling.

Things We Ask

He was found hanging in the hayloft
of his father's old barn. Not the Quonset
where they stored New Holland combines
for winter. The old barn. He'd put on a plaid work shirt
and his favourite Levi's. Everyone found out
the morning after Labour Day. *I can't explain*
anything today, our law teacher said.

So we wandered the halls. Second class:
Math. Fractions. White numbers
written on the blackboard. Pictured him
written in dust hovering above stale hay bales.
Dusk pouring in. Hands he somehow
tied together while he still existed
in rising dust, until he swayed
the slowest way, slower than lovers
in rowboats, slower than pendulums,
a subtle back and forth. At school,
a classmate walked in, back from the washroom,
her face stained with tears. They say he suffered
from a long illness. I wanted to know:
what compels you to climb that ladder,
then look at the loft below and step off – longingly – into darkness?

The Drive Home

We drive slow, our heads thick
as fog in October. Dripping into
our shit-box car like sap:

the dark. Our mothers
wait up, haloed in lamplight,
thinking of mangled cars

and tangled bodies.
We're dizzy from the drive,
stopping every few seconds

to pee or puke or both. The sky
is drenched in stars, our smoke-breath
sparkles in the cold.

Some of us keep hope folded
in our pockets. The rest
have held it up to lighters,

watched it turn to black,
then ash. We drink beer, hold
each other's damp hands,

but don't mind right here,
either, watching dawn crawl up
slowly from her prairie grave.

Her Own Fading Light

Harvest went on despite vanishing light.
Our dads traced dark fields in hundreds of lines.
Back then I waited for you every night.

Snow geese swooped slowly in synchronized flight,
each bird distinctive, common as shrines
reflecting the sun in fast-fading light.

The sharp blade of day saw us fight,
then you wept in the shade of the pines.
Back then I waited for you every night

while you fought with wheat infected with blight
as our dads scraped the earth in their combines.
(Harvest went on despite vanishing light.)

I once held your hand, admired the white
flesh that spread over a spray of blue veins,
back when I waited for you every night.

You did not speak as I walked out of sight
and read our dads' fields for any last signs.
Harvest went on despite vanishing light.
Back then I waited for you every night.

The Sky is Red

The sky is lentil red.
The sky is poppy-petal red.
The sky is red as his eyes after midnight.

The sky is red as his eyes after smoking two, maybe three, joints.
The sky is the red of your first period, staining the crotch of your thong
in the bathroom of your best friend's house, Grade 10.

The sky is red blood dampening the sepia hair
of a just-shot white-tailed buck in October.
The sky is red autumn.

The sky is red as wine.
The sky is red as his lips after eating the beet salad
the neighbours won't stop dropping off.

The sky is red as a robin's breast.
The sky is his red arms in springtime
after that first warm week in June working twelve-hour days
    under unobscured sun.

The sky is a scarlet red cow's heart displayed
in a butcher's case on parchment paper.
The sky is red as Heinz ketchup.

The sky is red as Cover Girl lipstick some brave girl
might've slid on before driving out to a barn party.
The sky is red as a bible cover.

The sky is red as the words that Jesus might've said.
The sky is red as the poinsettias your mother displayed in her kitchen
every Christmas.
The sky is purple-red and runny, the insides of Saskatoon berry pie.

The sky is flaking red paint, peeling off of falling-down barns
like skin after a bad burn.
The sky is glossy red, a Ford truck, freshly washed.

The sky is red as the tent you shared with the boy you liked
and your mutual friend. While you pretended to sleep, he fingered her.
The sky is red as the pen your science teacher used to write 33% at the
top of your Physics test.

The sky is red as the bricks of the Wilson Centre in Sedley, where
Social Services
once sent girls who broke the law. They escaped regularly.
The sky is the red Bohemian beer label you scraped off with
bitten-down nails.

The sky is your red tongue, thinking of something to say.
The sky is red – either love or humiliation.
The sky is red. The sun is setting.

As snow sends sleep

In the Morning

We live in lines now, on pages
snow falls slow and steady

as sleep, softly as crane feathers.
Softly as crane feathers, snow falls slow

from a midnight-ink sky I could dip
the tip of my pen in, write whichever ending

I choose from the last two years. The one where
I drag my pen over the coral-heart curve of your lips.

We used to kiss with open eyes. Yours
were a cold shade of pasture in morning mist.

A cold shade in mist. I learn this
is how you write a poem: run your tongue over it

10,000 times. Relentless. An open wound,
chipped tooth. Something almost senseless.

(Living)

We live in a hunk
of house, on land that seeps through
trees and leggy skies.

He comes home every
night, every nail a dust-brown
moon he scrubs away

with soap and sponge. He sighs
at limp, homemade perogies.
His mom used to roll

stiff dough for hours while
hundreds of women pinched them
into pale purses

for a mash of cheese
and bacon and potato.
I pinch, never roll.

Mornings he studies
pears, their plump swell of belly.
I tend to the toast,

touch my own flat flesh.
He dreams wheat and John Deeres,
hums the loose hush

of wind, the rush of
sudden rain. I recite
lines from travel guides.

(Dreaming)

I live in a small,
single room, a patchwork square
in this light-grey-light

apartment tower.
Strings of yellow cabs
hung with red, bright beads. People

snake through traffic stopped,
click across concrete
every New York night.

I eat slick slices
of salami-studded pies
bought from sidewalk men.

My bed holds only
the curve and sweet shampoo smell
of myself. That's fine.

(I recite lines I might set down tomorrow.)

happens at the theatre. We embrace and I am panicked-calm,
a mouse wrapped in a snake, my small sparrow heart rattling

its cage. You've always smelled like oil, dirt,
lentils spoiled, and I see a husk forgotten, caught in a lock

of your hair. I want to ask about the woman behind you
because she is beautiful and staring with eyes like Lake Louise.

But my tongue is stiff, a bleached carp, plump carcass
on pebbled sand. I bend down to pick it up, trip

into the water. And you are French braiding my hair the way
your sisters taught you. And you are carving out the feathery bones

of jackfish on your counter. And you are whipping brown sugar
and flour into a soft syrup, offering me the spoon.

And you drive your boat through a ditch the summer
all of Saskatchewan floods and everyone thanks God

for crop insurance. And you read out loud to me,
your tongue stumbling. (You say *Sorry* and I say *I don't mind*

but I do a little.) And you show me a photograph
of your mother who died of cancer in the same hospital

you were born in, bones poking through papery sheets,
her stomach a hollow bowl you could drink from.

And you are undressing me in the middle of your cold kitchen.
And you are undressing me trembling as a rabbit caught wild

in the long grass of the graveyard near town.
(We are hidden by windows grey with frost,

pale lacy ferns pressed onto the glass.)
And you are kissing goose bumps across my collar bone.

And you drag me, dead-heavy and drenched,
from the lake you showed me how to fish in, back to shore.

For my mother's skin

thin as petals, woven
with wrinkles, life's inevitable thread.

Feather-smooth once, touched
by my father, reckless as a twig

in a river. He left her swollen, bud
of flesh that split to give me a sip

of her life. Her hands reached down
to that torn seam of skin and felt a shock of hair

not her own. She trembled the first time
she held me, thought I looked like him –

eyes gold-round as chickpeas.
Her fists might clench tight as cherry pits, or lie

loose as breath. She could poke thread
through a hole smaller than an ant's eye,

pinch perogies into the plump curve
of half-hearts. She reminds me.

We are shaky, then certain; certain,
then shaky. We love, then do not.

We do not love,
then we love.

Lizzy

Vodka poured in mason jars veiled
in frost. *Queens*, they call us,

since we snob our noses
at warm-room beer in plastic cups.

Antlers line the walls
like bare-boned hands. Deer, moose, elk,

gunned down, gunned down
for sausage, jerky, dog food.

Her cheeks are late-day prairie
pink. We sneak a skinny joint

from her guy's truck, smoke-share
it in the bathroom,

pry up the pane.
A crack of cold air slips in.

Her kids lie in cribs
at home with a high school sitter.

A mess of curls, she laughs, clutching
her third vodka-seven. She used to

barrel race on a quick, black horse
called Blaze, before the second

babe. She's felt the sharp,
slow slice of birth, kidney stones.

She's peed on sticks, hoped for
life that lies in two lines.

When I sit on porcelain,
I pray blood drops.

We Knew

not to fear the night that held us
to itself, hummed us to sleep
with the crickets.

We knew David's dad drank too much –
not in a mean way, just in a soft, lost way.
Every night alone in the cold concrete

of his detached garage, clinging to a bottle
of draft in one hand, cigarette in the other
to cast himself out of there.

We knew when we saw storm clouds,
swirl of sky over canola,
we were really seeing something.

We knew in the end we'd forgive ourselves
for the torture, times we told the whole school
Angie got her period in class, Jay put cover-up

on his acne, I looked like a rodent, all cheeks and teeth.
We knew about winter, that if you tried
to walk home full of rye and lay down – hush

of snow sending sleep, under a sparkling ceiling
of two trillion stars – you wouldn't get frostbite,
you'd die. We knew Brandon's brother went organic,

not because he cared about being green, eating clean
or anything. He couldn't pay his chemical bill anymore,
couldn't pull in big yields, couldn't keep up.

We knew prairie could pin you
down to the ground like a graveyard cross,
so some of us couldn't leave, even if we wanted to.

Knew sometimes, we loved being 13 kids
living 13 years together, that knowing
left unsaid. We began to see that death

walks steadily forward, doesn't rush or get tired,
just walks endlessly, calmly. And when it eventually
heads right toward you, most are too scared to look.

The rain, cold and slow

Although That Town

is cupped in a soft palm, where a cluster of homes sit like seeds
at a sunflower's centre, it could never be the place I remember.

If I lift the green and gold, I remember some guys said they'd hang
the faggot in the grade below us. And we all tossed words –

retard, cunt – as casually as we tossed baseballs after class.
I see the Grade 11 girl who told me, a tender-scared thirteen,

with teeth-too-big and glasses, that I was the ugliest
girl she'd seen. What's a fresh teen to do, but believe her?

Still, some moments settled smooth as cream. Kristy and I washed
her Chevy
in the creek for free. Suds slid down its red sides, then floated,

drifts of shimmer-snow. The April air still held a winter hand,
so I sat only on stones the sun slept on. And goose bumps rose regardless.

Seventeen

You had a thing for catching baby
animals. I think you wanted to prove

you were good, a capable farm boy.
I was the useless town kid.

We saw that mama cow in the pasture
plodding behind her brown

and white baby, his newborn hair
wavy and damp. The grass

was rain-laced (or was it afterbirth?).
Rain, I'm sure of it. The sky had spread

moments earlier. A deep, dark blue, punched
out by pairs of clouds. I remember

that now. We plowed through
pasture and you walked right up

to the calf, scooped him, squeezed his hooves
together at the bottom, a brown bouquet.

The calf, fresh, one long bead
of placenta still stretched off his belly.

And everything smelled
of cattle and rain.

A Horse Named Breeze

Pinto or a Paint, depending on who you asked,
he had what looked like a map of the world

on his back: white continents and sepia seas.
Breeze was owned by my father's farmhand

but lived in the yard, in a pen
with no grass in it. He grazed a halo

around himself and sometimes slipped his head
between the bars, tried to sneak a few blades

just out of reach. Tom, his owner, was tall and thin
and the first cowboy I'd ever seen. (We didn't live

in the loose dirt of cattle country.) I liked Tom,
but I liked Breeze better, pretended he was my own,

imagined walking beside him (no halter
or rope between us) through a pasture – a lace-frost

veil drawn over the grass – in that pre-dawn
tracing-paper light, trying to make sense of the map

draped over him and the grass surrounding
us, all the stems bending the same way.

One Way to Die in Saskatchewan

1.

Gravel road flooded.

Slip-skid toward
a slough swelled
with Spring's icy

child, steel and
wintry water. You

should think about
breaking glass, buckles

and every sucked
breath, but don't. Twelve hours

later, a hand touches you

too late, diver discovers death
already painted you

pale dress
floats thin

as a fish fin and tightly
curled snails hover

around you

like watery stars.

2.

Truck plunges, you remember
the buckle, the breath, to break

the glass and as steel
plows, you flee
ribbon-limbed

but determined.
Hair unfurled like drenched

petals. Shudder

onto clear
hard road
as something like

pale paint stains
the water around you.

Too tired to stand
pant, suck every breath

until a stranger stops
presses one hot hand

against your forehead.
Seems like ages since you felt
flesh, yours

or someone else's.

The Pearl

In the front yard: fuchsia
petunias, a hummingbird
flitting in between
thin leaves. Perhaps I'm the receipt

tossed around the dust-flooded
dashboard, then sucked
out the window. (Below smooth skin
there are ripples.) If you like, pour

me into a cheap china tea cup,
lacy-floral as Valentine's Day.
Hover above until your face
is damp-warm as a washcloth.

Spring wind spreads
like a fever, forces everything
inside. Don't take me home, tie
gingham strings tight

around my waist. Don't place the towel
in my hands, rest your head in the slope
between my shoulder and my throat,
press me up against the sink's edge

a few moments. Show me the egg
in the palm of your hand – pale-slick
and round as a pearl. The sky
cracks open and rain runs down

thick as yolk. Go outside
(it's been dry) and stand in it,
even though it's freezing –
early April – and you shiver.

Jake

He is dead now longer than he lived.
His graduation photo is printed at the front
of an old high school yearbook and etched

on his gravestone. With his slicked hair,
suit and straight teeth, he looks like a teenaged CEO.
His father's name carved after his first name.

His mother writes a memoriam for him
every year. Tried walking home from the city
bar one night. Drunk, he lay down. A farmer found him

in his field, few days later, frozen. Eighteen. Everyone asks,
Where were his friends? The ones he grew up with,
who scored beside him, under banners stamped

with their fathers' names. The boys who walked him to school,
teased him first time his voice cracked, who sat laughing
beside him in bonfire light, sucking on cigarettes whose cherry tips

drooped like plump tulips in the soft, steady heart of night.
Maybe those boys left him, sick of his lulling tongue,
bittersweet breath. Some say the cops took him

on a starlight tour, picked him up, slurring his steps
on a busy street, then dumped him outside city limits.
He felt cold that last night, must have. But perhaps

there was a moment when cold seeped out and earth curled
around him. And the mud-luscious scent
of her hair was everywhere, until he slipped into sleep, tasting

the soil that soaked the lines of his father's fingers
during harvest, the salty palms of his mother's hands,
the leather of his baseball glove, the morning mist.

Graduation

Build house, career, right here.
New season of settlers – their wives and TVs overseas
in Pakistan or Ireland – who haven't come to seed flat land
by hand. We are too young
to know change in this place.
Promise pours into *new Saskatchewan*,
but we no longer ponder potash. Only think of oil
if the neighbours build a pool or buy brand-new.
Thousands of jobs. More bodies than ever. More than a million.
This is what we've done:

All we know is the price of land
and lentils. Most of us squeezed
our dreams then let go.
They are lying beside the dugout.
Some believe the best has left us, even though
our faces are still smooth as spoons.
First summer out, we'll move into shacks quivering
like canola on the edge of town, clutch jobs on rigs,
the pipeline, wherever money's strewn.
We know what's coming, and too soon.

Know someday not far away, we'll all live tick-tock
ho-hum day-to-day. Some still texting high school loves
who remind us of times we lay on the hoods
of second-hand trucks, our summer breath thick
as whiskey, warm as grain bin dust. Nights
our sticky hands and foreheads felt like flu.

When we felt each other's tongues
and couldn't believe how damn lucky we were
that all our parents wanted were live bodies in bed by 2:00.
Wondering what we should do –

eventually buy that new 500 horsepower Ford Raptor?
Some of us want out of new Saskatchewan:
already had enough of winter curled up
and cold, a dead foal. Some escape and answer
to bosses; others stay,
sentenced to houses. New wife
changing diapers alone while the dog barks.
Is it enough to tend
children and wade through Red Fife
with this one fragile, singular life?

The Garden

My fingers settle.
Your lips, moth wings
on Lady Slippers.

Whisper this
story full of rain.
Feel it:

that easy breath.
My hand
across your arm,

now cool and slick.
I want to drink these nights
straight from cupped palm.

Find it, the soft wave of hip
and glide over,
tender study of skin.

We want only
the shape, gentle scrape
of each other.

Party

Mondays will be different
from now on. After thirteen years
we will return home to curl under
childhood sheets – old pillows

held to ears like conch
shells – one last time. At the last
party we cling, swarm like flies
around the sticky mouths

of each other, forgive what we flung
in anger in the daytime. We hold
the night folding slowly
as a fan. Grab vodka,

bitter-hot, share a j inside
the Quonset, floor stained
with spilled stories, warm
beer. *Chels, are you drunk*

yet? No, I'm actually not even drunk,
honest to God. We memorize
the unsteady pulse
of one another. Gentle

push, sudden weight
of hands, silky eyelids.
Silently lying:
we will always be friends.

Time wrinkled as a fan,
waves us softly away from
each other. Thrum of night, lazy hum.
Unsteady pulse of one.

You Taught Me

how to pull northern pike
through that lake's glossy lips

how to tear bodies firm as fists
through her rippling skin.

You laid them in your boat's bottom,
swearing: *You dumb sonofabitch. You little dick.*

That thing is so far down. But skilled,
you swivelled out every hook

as their strong bodies squirmed, every scale
aching for that lake to take them. Gills flared,

brilliant fans, and when you slipped them in
they took off in one smooth ribbon swerve.

Your hands sliced and bleeding
from teeth and fishing line.

Up north a pike gulped my hook,
thin curl of blade wrapped up

in gut. Soaked in lake spit
he almost slipped through my fingers.

I tried to coax it out quick as he twisted,
slim and strong as a wrist, fins thin-stiff

as feathers. But soon blood swirled
over my skin, his scales, so I tugged out

the hook in three quick rips and threw him in.
His body bobbed, up and down in his own crimson cloud.

That morning full of fog; rain fell cold
and slow. I pictured you, shivered, pulled up anchor.

Not a Farm

He called her pretty
funny and that was the first time

she heard a boy call someone he liked
something other than pretty. He wanted

a farm: something far away and a barn
for her horse. That's it. She wanted – not a farm

or a barn far away from the light of the city.
Not a horse grazing under a sky soaked in starlight.

(Later she sleeps in the city under an orange-fog sky
that hovers above houses at night. He sleeps

in a hundred-year-old house under the long wing
of night.) She thinks of him in his yard

where he drives around in a John Deere tractor, cuts grass,
hundreds of laps. He has a few more wrinkles

around his eyes. A few, that's it. She walks across
his yard in the rain, walks over wrinkled soil.

He and this soil are almost the same
as the summer she left. His eyes are the same

hazel: a horse's mouth after grazing on pasture grass.
Pasture grass after rain: hazel, grazing, just the same.

Rural Hangover

God, I was slim then – walking in,
stripping down, lying down

in that dirt-morning
light, hungover, and nausea tucked

under my mind like an old note.
I didn't mind those mornings: click

of dried contacts, tumbleweed
stomach and the sun pouring

through bedroom windows.
Before the farmhouse,

you lived in a trailer
with walls so thin, I swear

you could see through them.
Hardly a yard, just pasture, and cattle

peering in, curious as trick-or-treaters.
You woke early to work: feed cows,

move bales, study seed openers. The rhythm
of heavy equipment lumbering around

in the background, behind an alarm clock
song, low volume. Held between that

scribble of tin, we loved each other
while dust fell, silver

and squinting – leftover
confetti, dead and then reanimated again.

Flatlander

    Before seeding but after the snow melts
you run the gravel road that leads
    out of town. Pencil-lead sky:
gold stubble glows sharp
    against the grey. The way the land is.
You watch rain in the distance
    hurl itself toward earth. The way it reaches you.
It covers and reveals like a journal like a veil.
    Everything slows
holds its breath for a moment:
    you the geese the frogs. And you run
through it run through until
    your white bra shows up under
your white shirt. Hope nobody
    drives by. Here there is blank space.
No rivers lakes no trees just dugouts one single
    thin creek. The sky writes something
down pours itself into the driest ground
    it can find. When everything dries out again
you'll make sparrow tracks in the dust
    with a stick smooth over your own footprints
with the palm of your hand.
    Hide yourself from this flat land.

Everything reflects the electric sun

[S]outhern Saskatchewan received only 50% of normal precipitation and recorded one of its hottest summers ever…the 1986-88 drought also triggered staggering losses (e.g., a $4 billion drop in grain exports) to Canadian agriculture. – Encyclopedia of Saskatchewan

1988

The summer I am born, the soil splits
wide open: chapped as winter lips,
a faded mosaic, dirt quilt. Sun

sucks up dugouts, ditches, creeks.
Calves collapse and coyotes
tear flesh from the bodies.

There is neither rain nor money.
Mothers go back to work.
Lawyers drive down farm lanes

through a greasy heat you can see,
demanding land and signatures
from men with dark, cracked faces.

The sun can be hungry, but imagine
answering to anyone else. You know one day
she'll lead you out to a field so gold-soft,

you'll worry it's a mirage until you brush
your hands over braided heads
and remember wind mixed with wheat

sounds like whispering and rain. But that summer,
the sun swells bright, a poisonous bloom
in a sky you wish you could tip to your lips and drink from.

Sedley

Thin slip of earth buried
under a July sky so clear-blue
you could bathe in it. But slim

surfaces deceive. Beneath
is damp, black soil, the kind
farmers fall to their knees for.

They cradle it in their palms,
inhale the scent of its velvety flesh.
It's the type of soil a man claws at

with his bare hands
after three broke, hungry years
to find one tiny seed – no larger

than a pearl – with one green, thin curl
bursting from it.
It's a place where everything reflects

the electric sun and some people
hide from it.
This is where I'm from.

This place: a few hundred somebodies
who know what it means to bet everything
on the sky.

The Farmyard

That childhood, threadbare
and faded from the rub of my own body.
The bones of my first cat – buried under a fir tree
in the farmyard my father still regrets selling.
Plains stretched thin as an apron.
Land licked clean as a plate.
Fields wide and wavering
as linen on my mother's clothesline.
That first Seven-up mixed
with vodka in a plastic pop bottle.
The first time I got drunk, one midnight
in June, at the baseball diamond, with girls
I once sat next to, sounding out words.
A snowy owl's long, slow swoop –
a vole in his talons.
A frog folded up in the palm
of my hands like a poplar leaf
or an olive heart, softly beating.
More than wild
life, bright and sudden, stumbling in,
it was the firm tug of tomorrow
on the end of the line.

The Push

When school let out
for the summer, she was alone.

Hours piled up as she walked the gravel
behind the family farmyard, sweat forming along

her pearly-cream throat. He stopped
one time late in the day – his rusty Chevy drove

them to some place forgotten by everyone.
Peeled back clothes, discarded each cotton skin.

Truck cab damp as the afternoon, overgrown honeysuckle,
hush of wind, sky stretched thin as a moth wing.

He pushed her head among the steady mosquito hum,
disheartened thrum of tongue, the farmhouse nearby,

time's firm thumb pressing it back to the ground.
Spiders laid claim, laced the place in cobwebs, gold-silk

glimmer in dying light. The last smoky sun slipped
through his cracked truck window. He dropped her off

at the four-way closest to her farm. She hurried home,
her pale pear flesh all goose bumps.

She didn't know for sure the feeling:
lonely or just alone.

Ball Park at Midnight

In the dark, we sit in the diamond,
run fingers over the red braids
of baseballs as if they are braille.
Glance at our nails painted
Sally Hansen teal, wait

for the empty days ahead
to fill. Pass plastic bottles full
of vodka, try not to spill, recall
the time Cody read out loud:
"chicken co-op" instead of coop.

The nights to come a certain hum
in the distance. Discuss Mr. Duffy,
what makes him sexy (he's a poor man's
Wayne Gretzky). Wait for the empty days
ahead to fill. We read each other better

than the red seams of baseballs:
know who shoplifts, who asks
girls to email shots of themselves topless,
who wears air-filled bras, terrified
someone will brush up against her.

A certain hum in the distance.
The nights to come will drain the wild
from us, leave us stunned –
nights in the diamond slipped away
quick as deer in wheat fields in the dark.

Minors

When we lived together, each day spread
wide as a wishbone. Cow-eyed, I survived,
cracked into apples for fun, just to feel

something tender bend, something ripe burst.
Lunch: spaghetti, meat sauce,
lemon dish liquid on fingertips. My skin

pale-smooth, sliver of soap left behind.
Your skin stained bronze. And some days rain-
braided peonies pooled like marbles,

the drops reflecting our own faces.
When it poured, we hid
in the bar where boys hoping

to inherit the family farm wished on the freckles
of nineteen-year-old girls gulping hard iced teas,
the ones who last year sat on Co-op steps drinking

Coke. Three a.m. we emerged to wisps of rain, wet
smoke uncoiling from the street. The air, damp
as a cherry, sweet as the mouth of a past love.

That Summer

1.

He wanted to build a house out of something
sturdy – brick or stone, maybe – for his future wife.

His wife should have been the girl he took
to his school dance, the one with blond hair,

a bow-tie waist. He said she always wanted a kitchen
full of bread-and-baby-powder smells, plush cheeks

to cup her hands around, a diamond – tiny one, even –
shiny eye to stare up at her always. Morning coffee

with other wives and a husband, handsome, whose hands
held her, but also seeds and black soil.

2.

When we met, he still wanted the farmhouse.
He stood, strong and tall, describing his late mother:

she cooked, butchered chickens,
kept a spotless house. Cleaned only with bleach.

I left him years later, the summer after
Saskatchewan flooded, but I pretend I left

the summer before. When everything gleamed
green as Ireland. Rain streamed down window panes,

glowed in grass, hung lights in poplars. It ripped through roads,
flooded farm lanes. All summer, farmers cursed

more than usual. He begged me to stay,
but I was scared of life reliant

on skies. The bare blue of so many summers.
The low, rolling grey of that summer.

The First Light and The Last

They gripped brand-new life in strong, small fists.
Slipped in, like pickerel, all eyes and slick
lips, tasting her skin in quick, small sips.

First drink: warm and thick,
not as warm as the womb, but they liked it.
First glimpse: her long, blond hair, her skin

soft as a blossom. She raised them all
in a farm house, long forgotten,
on a small plot of land not near any water.

One of those babies, my father's father,
flew planes until he grew wheat.
He gripped life tight in sinewy fists, until the last

fluorescent-lit minute, the green glow
of the hospital: unlike the first light,
that farmhouse washed white,

the crabapples, pink and ripe and right outside;
casting shadows on her bedroom wall, dappled
as an Appaloosa. In that light, he slipped in.

Homecoming

My mother calls the Sedley Hotel, crumbled hunk of bar that sits
on town's rim, bloated as an old boat. She asks for my father.

It is August 20th, 1988, and the land is dry and pale
as paper. Never a cloud, not even a wisp of cirrus. Every night

is the same and tonight is no exception: starry, cloudless, full moon
a radiant flame. Barmaid says he's not there

(that he told her to say that) and hangs up. She scratches
her striped belly swell, second beating heart. My foot stuck

into it like a cookie cutter. My parents' house is new: beige paint
and plush peach carpet. Crickets cry out in the concrete

basement. Electric fan shakes its head "no" over and over, slowly,
in one corner of the kitchen. She waddles out to the year-old Camaro

(sloppy on gravel; she rolled it driving 40 klicks an hour)
she'll be forced to sell once I'm here. Drives, windows all the way

down to let in the foggy evening air, steady bug lullaby. Strolls in,
confident as a coyote, belly sticks out way past her jean jacket,
    belly button

pops through her tee shirt. *You* – pointing at my father – *get your ass out of that chair right now. Baby's coming. Smarten up. I'll drive.*

The Getaway Car

Post-midnight, Saskatchewan summer:
we listen to our own damp breath
and lightning-thunder air panting outside

open windows. Study lines in the landscape
for cherry-blue flashes. The cops, we hope,
are a long way off. On our way home

from the only bar in town –
not drunk and not sober – we've stopped.
In the middle of wheat fields, we might be criminals

but we feel more like heroes in this living hour.
Everyone has a story about outrunning Mounties.
This is ours, helped along by the thick whispering

of insects in a nearby lagoon, and stillness.
The dark suffocates and sustains so we can't tell
if these are our last few breaths, or the first.

Ms. Williams

She lies crumpled
as a sheet
in a grassy ditch between
gravel and canola.
The boy hit her

on his way to work.
The first responders
try to save her, CPR, mouth-
to-mouth. But it is not a day
for saving. They ignore

her quickly cooling skin, the dirt
and the flies. These grown men:
sweat, dust, watery eyes.
Her shirt torn off and

farmers stopping to help
or gawk. Scent of pennies
mixed in with late-summer
sun and eventually the moment.

When Benjamin comes, he dives down
to her, holds up her heavy head
and wails. Her life

stopped.
He shakes her, shakes her,
shakes her, as if it might
wake her up.

As he cries, he prays.
Her eyes are still open.

The boy sits, can't look
at this woman who
taught him school.

This will be one of those moments,
a stone he places carefully
in his pocket, one that rubs
against his body always –

before he falls asleep and again
when he wakes up, when he walks
across the stage at graduation,
in the grocery store, in the car,
at the doctor's office with his
new daughter.

When my dad calls to tell me
about Ms. Williams, I am standing
on our back deck.

I look out past the fields, shimmery
skins. The land, vast and bare
as birth, has its own way
of obscuring. I can't see the accident.

The sky drags its fingers across the spine
of the prairies, over every ridge,
every bump, the dust

rising behind her car like steam
off a colt as she drives to work, windows
cracked, sunlight – dime-bright – sliding in,

radio singing hits, cherry air freshener swinging
and summer so ripe she can taste it, the salt
and the dirt and the heat of it. No school,

nobody's mother, just a job at the seed plant
to keep her and her husband in groceries
until the fall.

Breath in August

Side by side in the box of the old Ford
you plan to trade in, we lie under blankets
with cherry whiskey.
Your hair's covered in dust

and I taste the Saskatoon berries
you ate under a cloudless blue
moment this afternoon. Here: spilled lentils,
crickets, grasshoppers, damp. The fields are hard

and black as horse hooves,
the night scraped bare.
We talk. You will not leave
the farm. One day it's yours. I wonder

if I should stay home, learn to cook, and you say: *No,*
I've seen you happy here, but never seen you content.
Here: spilled lust, limbs, velvet breath, wet.
And some faraway train that rips through night.

Like a comet born in a shock of light, it moves
quickly and slowly at the same time,
then disappears – a body
in a coffin of soft soil, a dazzling corpse.

Late-Night Tulip

His face felt like a crop sown in silk dirt –
sharp stubble on freckled skin.
He was farmer-shy. I was the flirt.
He was thick, not fat. And I, plain, wisp-thin.

Sharp stubble on freckled skin,
I felt it one day when I leaned in close.
I saw him bottle-feed a black, too-thin
calf to stop the gun shot, the lethal dose.

I felt it one day when I leaned in close.
We lay side-by-side in the bed of his Ford.
We listened for a gun shot, the lethal dose.
To keep him close, I pretended to be bored.

We lay side-by-side in the bed of his Ford.
I touched his mouth. Like a late-night tulip, it stayed
softly closed. To keep him I pretended to be bored.
He ran his hand down the ripple of my braid.

I touched his mouth. Like a late-night tulip, it stayed
softly closed. I smiled. I was after all, the flirt.
With a seed of shyness, he touched the ripple of my braid.
His face felt like a crop sown in silk dirt.

After Farmers Spray For Grasshoppers

The air smells like a body in a hospital:
sweat and heavy breath, medicine.
The fields are scrubbed
clean, gleaming. Your father hates

gloves and masks, and when
he arrives home for beef stew,
he walks into the bathroom first
and vomits. Insecticide

dulls the hearts of living things.
The seed plant that used
to greet people on the outskirts
is torn down, the land sold

to a man who opened a salvage yard.
The high school closed in '07,
too few students. New farmers:
an ex-Calgarian; the son

of an ag equipment millionaire;
an oil and gas billionaire.
(Most couples retired
to double-wide trailers in Arizona.)

A coyote slips into a canola field.
The sulphur flowers swallow him.
Canola and sky left behind.
And the thin line separating them.

The Way Home

What I didn't know is that once love ends, it doesn't
leave, but follows just behind. Sometimes I forget
it's there, then stop, look over my shoulder.

We find a robin's nest on a grain truck.
I hold one of the eggs, marvelling at pale blue
on peach palm, its plumpness – the way it hides
small, steady hearts – its gentle curve.

Together, we enter a dark barn. Streams of light hang
in the rafters between the soft conversation of pigeons.
We watch a tabby lap water from a margarine tub,
sweep it up with her freckled-petal tongue.

Things end. It's like lentils spilled
inside a truck, but were cleaned up.
Years later, looking for a lost coin
on the mat, I grab something: lentils.

We stroke the noses of your neighbours' horses.
Suck up the salty-sweet musk of summer: hay, dust, sweat.
Yank up grass and let them eat it from our hands,
their mouths green and foamy with it, like the skin of a marsh.

Sometimes we watch a storm drag its feet through a pasture
full of black cattle, stirring up a watery broth
of thunder and rain, raspberries, crushed clover,
clouds. Sometimes we stand in it and back in the truck,
you pluck rain from my eyelashes.

Love follows like a familiar horse: head low,
slow, ears forward. It doesn't charge or
rear up, just plods behind, trusting
I know the way home.

Reckless

Unobstructed
sky opened wide as a bible
and wind slithering. In love
with the lull, a ballad

of grasshoppers and boreal chorus frogs –
a reckless stretch, we hoped, still lay ahead.
The catch: some of us
already sensed our epilogues.

We lay in wheatgrass and junegrass
when some still believed in outsmarting death
and crickets confessed without stopping.
Moonless sky and stars, still as the glass

in our mothers' coffee tables. First dew
dampened the backs of our hand-me-down
shirts while we studied the lights
on the outskirts until 2:00.

There were always more Augusts
until the last one arrived
like a burrowing owl, the bird they've tried to save
from disappearing into dust.

Lucky

Electric webs stretch
across the night.
Rain falls thick and sleek
as fur pelts. We are driving
back to your farmhouse
from a wedding, a school gym
reception: basketball nets
draped in white Christmas lights.

We pull over
to have sex in the back seat
of the F-350 you're still
making payments on.
Leather seats, floor mats
covered in dust and dog hair. A film
of our own breath on the windows.

Poplar branch canopy overhead.
Steady thundercloud pulse –
we press our hands
against the glass and read it.
You leave to take a piss
in the storm. Your brown hair
stands straight up in the gale
and it feels good to laugh
in that atmosphere, chaotic
and static, like the one long pause
before the groom lifts the veil.

Sedley/2

Sometimes you drive down Highway 33,
the pin-straight length of pavement

running past a town held between
gravel and flax flowers. That town lures you,

covers your face with the ether cloth: a biologist
pushing pins straight through silk wings, a meteorologist

mapping garter-snake wind before it slips away quickly,
cutting a path through dappled grass. But it's only

the sky, a handful of people you knew, a bit of earth
thin and essential as blood, your breath.

Notes

"Week One" takes a line from Laisha Rosnau's poem, "On The Ground." "Party" is written after her poem, "Point of Exit," and "The First Light and The Last"' is written after her poem, "The Girls Are Sleeping."

"Graduation" is written after Nathan Mader's poem, "'Moving Back to the Bakken Play."

"Homecoming" is written after Matt Rader's poem, "Exodus."

The poem, "Graduation," mentions Red Fife. Red Fife is Canada's oldest wheat variety. It was the dominant wheat variety in the country for years – before Marquis replaced it as the number one variety in Canada in the early 1900s. (Marquis was bred using Red Fife.) Red Fife is no longer a significant part of the Canadian agriculture industry and is not exported. However, farmers still grow it across the country, mostly organically.
http://www.thecanadianencyclopedia.ca/en/article/red-fife-wheat/.

Acknowledgements

Poems, some in earlier versions, appeared in *The Antigonish Review*, *Arc*, *CAROUSEL*, *CV2*, *The Dalhousie Review*, *Echolocation*, *EVENT*, *Grain*, *Qwerty* and *Spring*. I am grateful to the editors of each.

Some of these poems also made up the submission that was selected as the winner of the 2017 City of Regina Writing Award. Thank you to the judges, Ayesha Chatterjee and David Waltner-Toews. Thank you, also, to the City of Regina for the financial support.

A previous version of "The Fall" was longlisted for *CV2*'s 2016 Young Buck Poetry Prize and an earlier version of "The full moon, a yard light" was shortlisted for the same prize. Thank you to the judge, George Murray.

For all of your early encouragement: Thank you to my teachers, Mrs. Clifford, Mrs. Robertson and Ms. Deters.

For introducing me to poetry, for making me a better poet, for helping to shape this collection: Thank you to my professors, Gerry Hill, Medrie Purdham, Randy Lundy and Sheri Benning.

Bruce Rice, thank you for your careful reading of this collection. It is stronger and clearer because of your input.

Thank you, also, to everyone at Coteau Books for giving me this book. You have all treated me wonderfully.

Thank you to Jeff Nye for lending your beautiful artwork to the cover.

Most importantly, thank you to my family (Mom, Dad, Dylan)
and of course, Ken.

About the Author

Photograph by Stick Productions

Chelsea Coupal grew up in the village of Sedley, Saskatchewan and now lives in Regina, where she completed a Master of Arts degree in Creative Writing. She won the 2017 City of Regina Writing Award and was shortlisted for *CV2*'s 2016 Young Buck Poetry Prize. Her poetry has appeared in literary journals across Canada, including *Arc, CV2* and *Grain.*